SCHIRMER'S LIBRARY
OF MUSICAL CLASSICS

Vol. 1857

CLAUDE DEBUSSY

Petite Suite

En Bateau
Cortège
Menuet
Ballet

Piano, Four-Hands

Edited by
JOSEPH PROSTAKOFF

ISBN 978-0-7935-5111-8

G. SCHIRMER, *Inc.*

DISTRIBUTED BY
HAL•LEONARD®
CORPORATION
7777 W. BLUEMOUND RD. P.O. BOX 13819 MILWAUKEE, WI 53213

Petite Suite

Edited by Joseph Prostakoff

Claude Debussy

En Bateau
(Boating)

Secondo

Piano

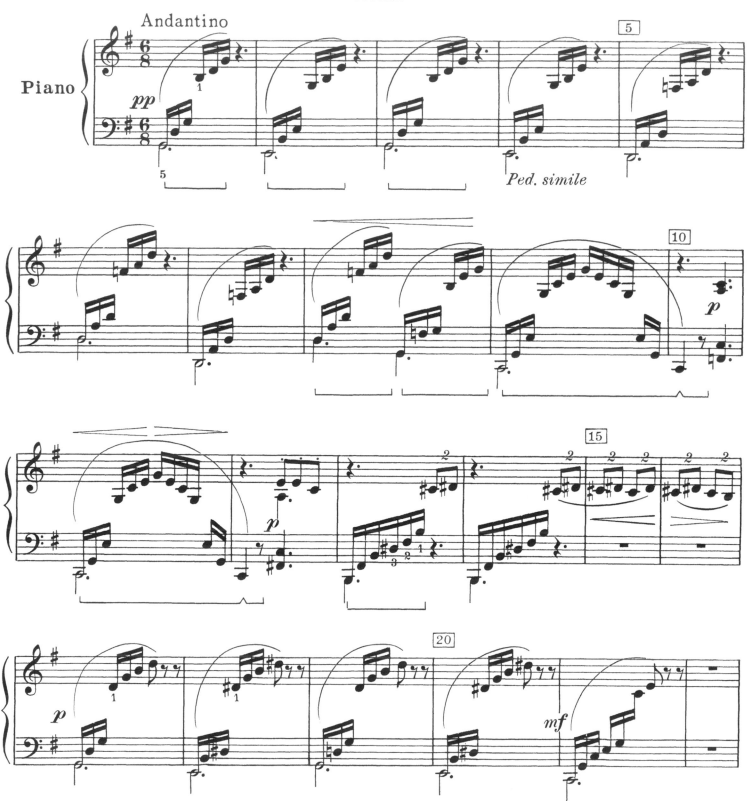

46266c

Petite Suite

Edited by Joseph Prostakoff

Claude Debussy

En Bateau

(Boating)

Primo

Secondo

Secondo

Secondo

Cortège

Cortège

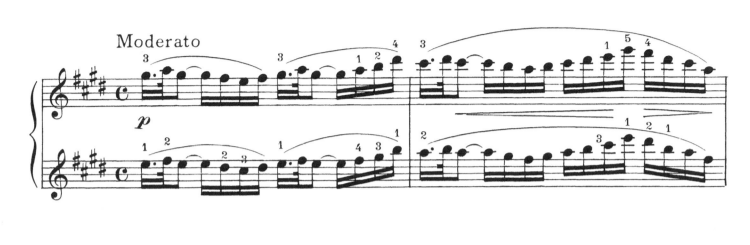

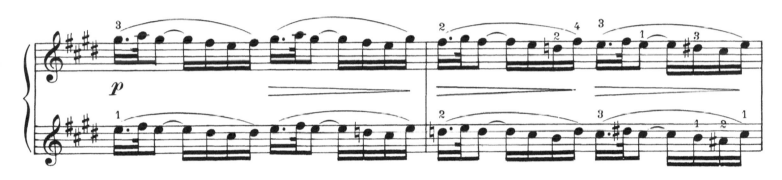

Secondo

Secondo

Secondo

Menuet

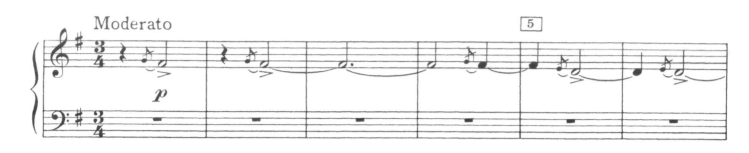

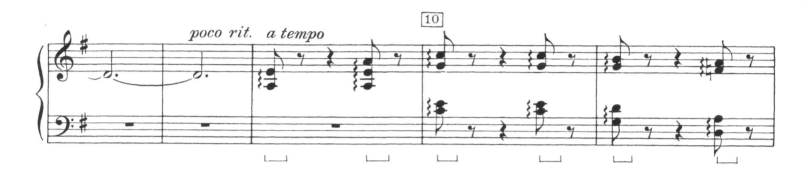

Menuet

46266

Secondo

Secondo

Ballet

Allegro giusto

Ballet

Secondo

Secondo

Secondo